The Tr

by Ruth Montgomery • illustrated by Sue Cornelison

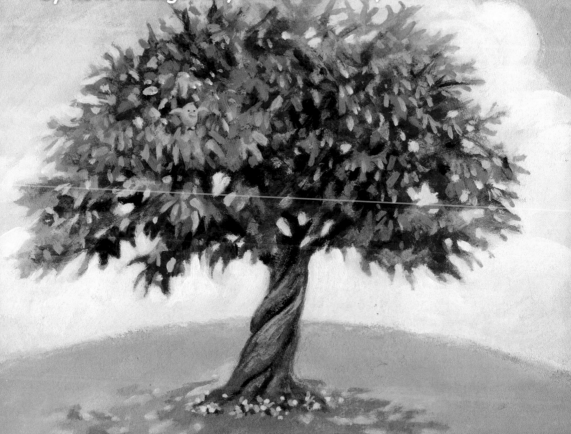

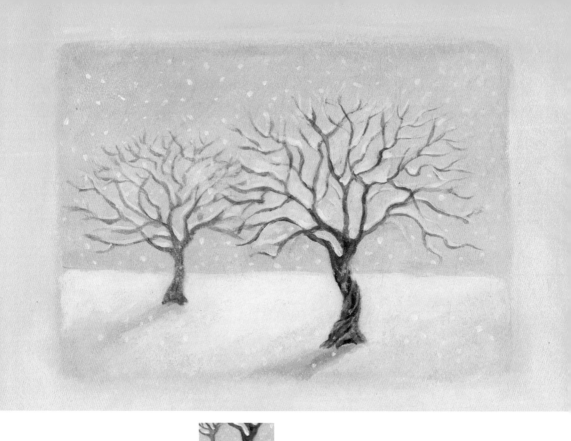

The 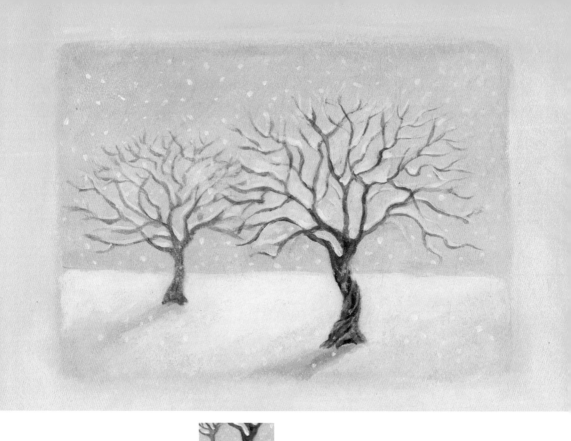 are big.

trunks

2

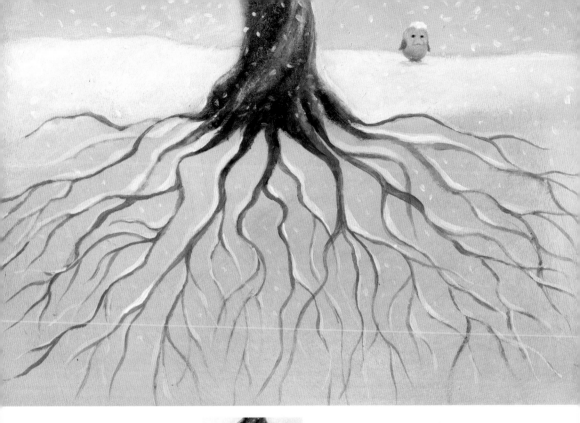

The 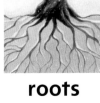 are big.

roots

3

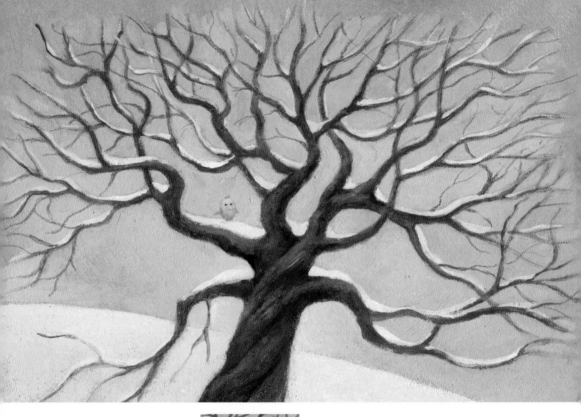

The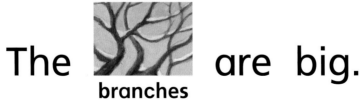
branches
are big.

4

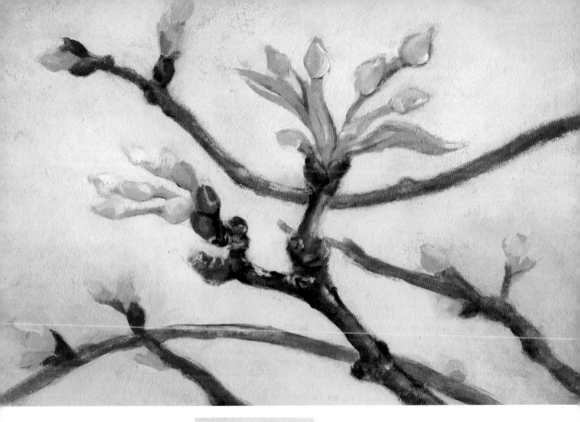

The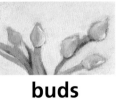
buds
are big.

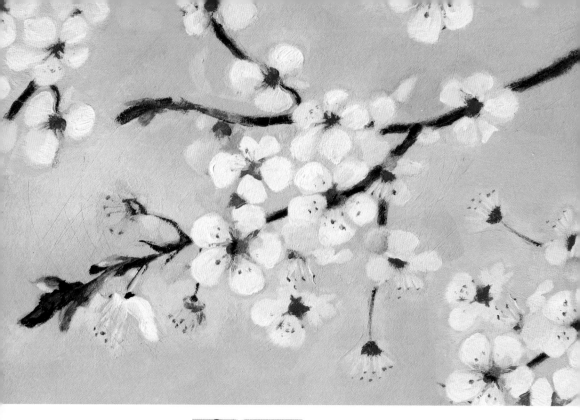

The 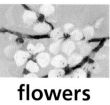 are big.

flowers

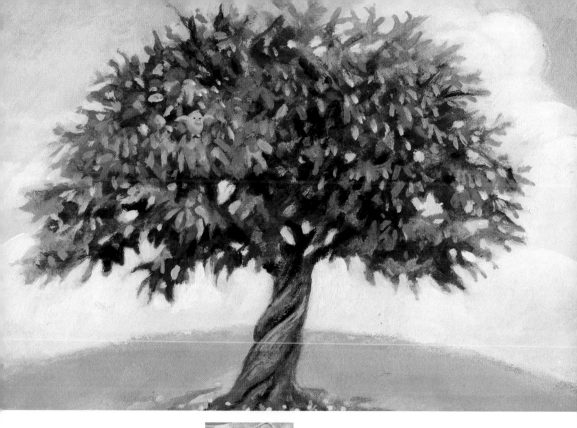

The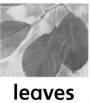
leaves
are big.

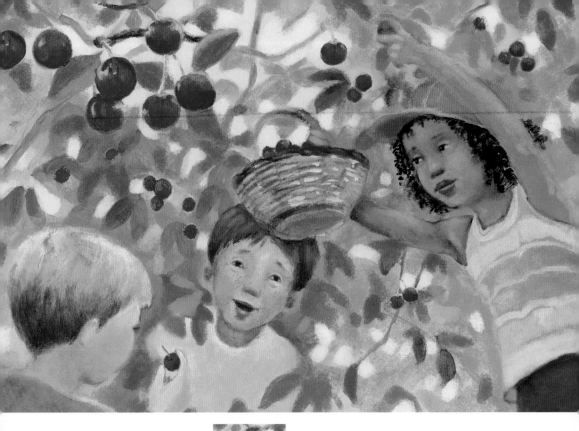

The are big.

cherries